DOODLES IN OUTER SPACE

ILLUSTRATED BY IRVÎN RAÑADA

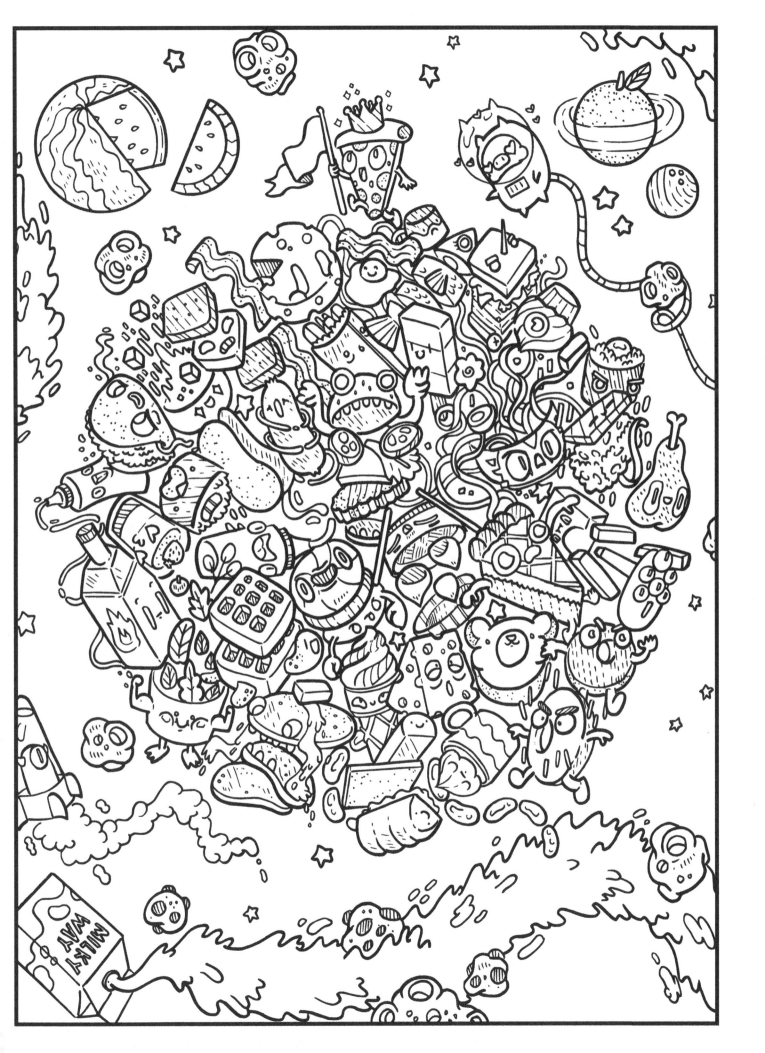

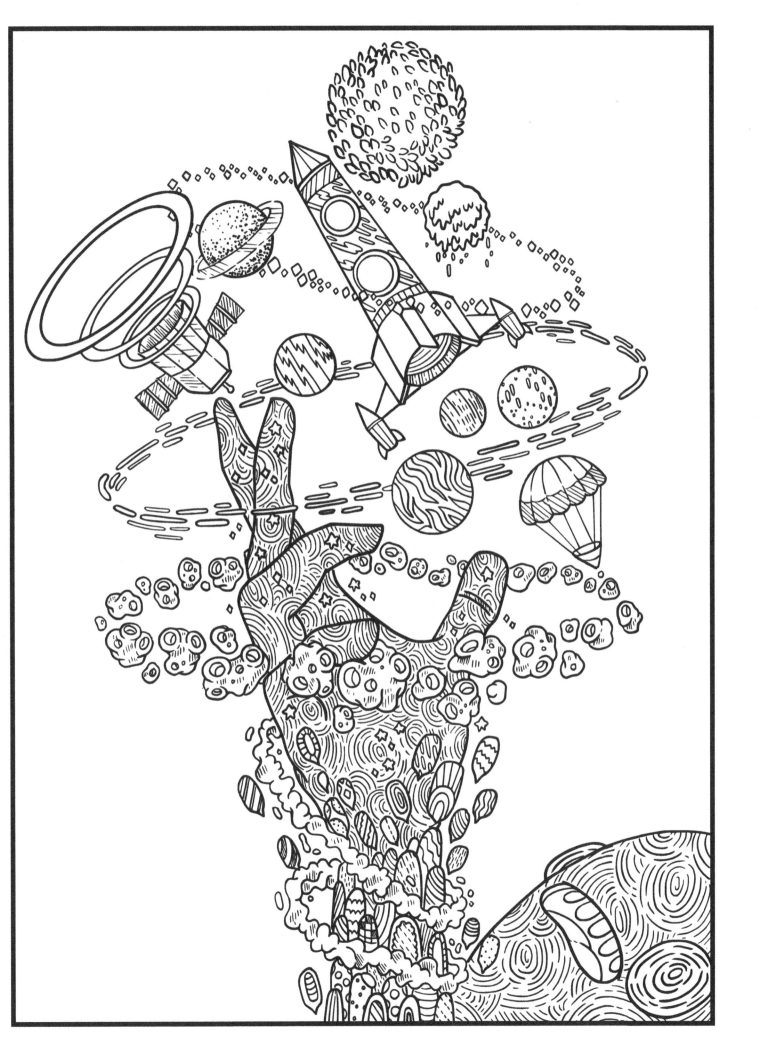

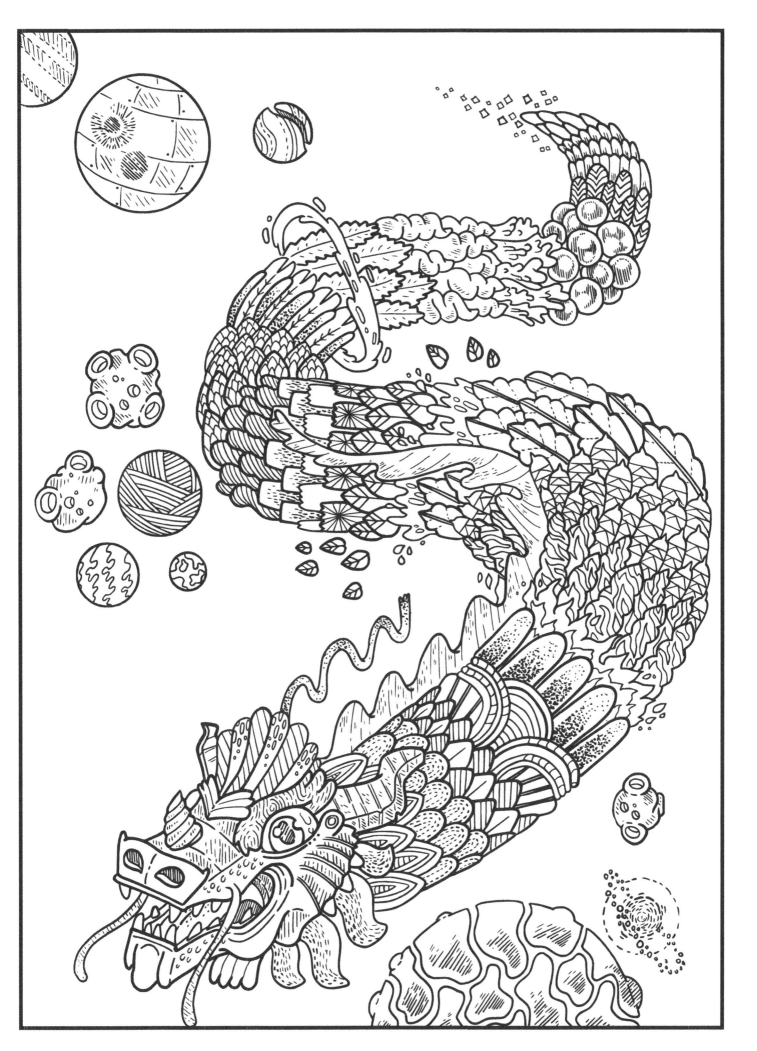

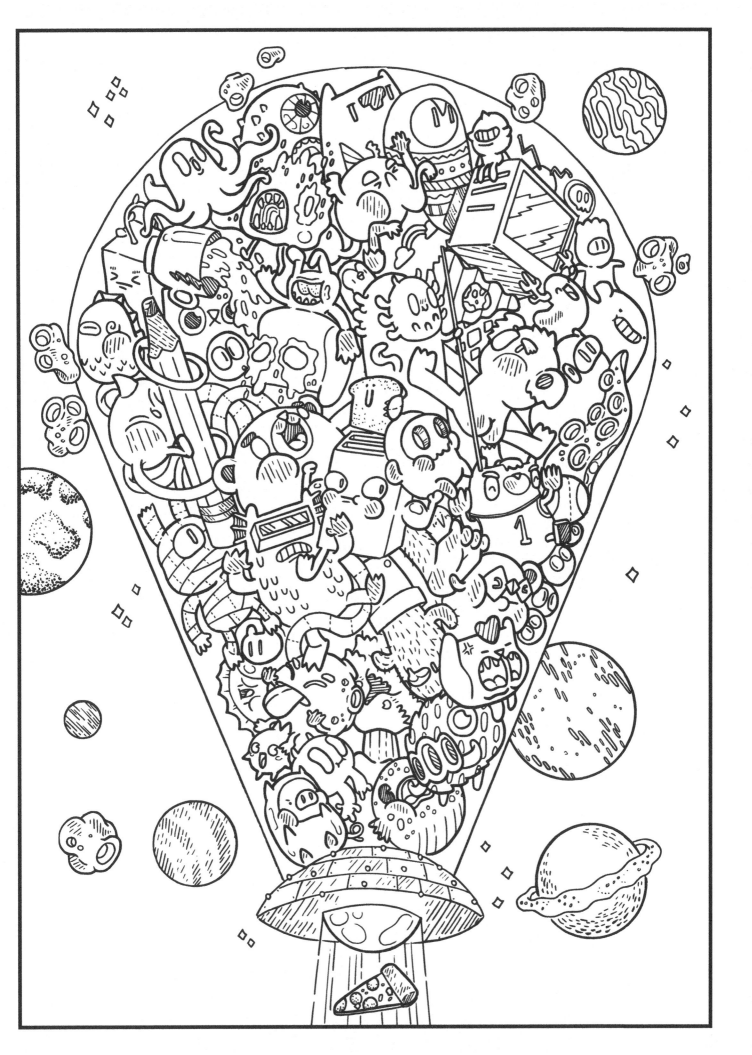

Coloring books from Okami Books

Subscribe to the newsletter to receive free coloring pages, as well as updates about upcoming promotions and free stuff.

www.okamibooks.com

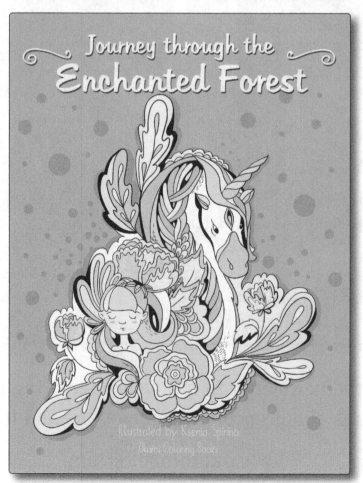

Celtic Inspirations

Okami Books

Illustrated by Veronika Fryziuk

Okami Books

Impressions of Spring

Illustrated by MgA. Radana Planka

International Delicacies

Illustrated by Ksenia Spirina

Okami Coloring Books

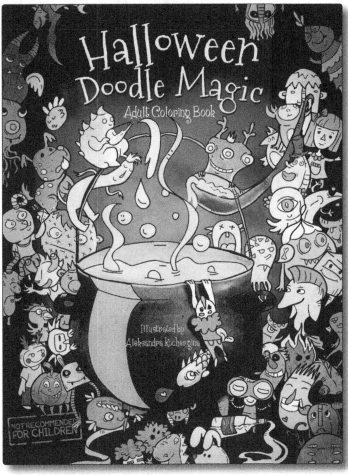

Halloween Doodle Magic

Adult Coloring Book

Illustrated by
Aleksandra Kochergina

Okami Books

NOT RECOMMENDED FOR CHILDREN

Children's books from Okami Books

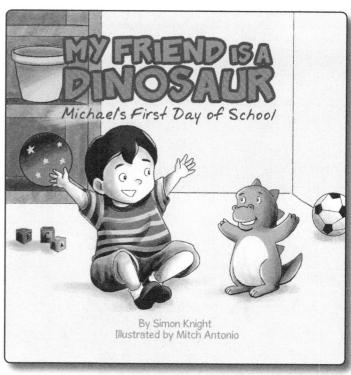

Subscribe to the newsletter to receive free coloring pages, as well as updates about upcoming promotions and free stuff.

www.okamibooks.com

Made in the USA
Las Vegas, NV
11 August 2023

75950364R00050